THINK ON

THESE THINGS

Inspirational Thoughts with Scripture

Whatsoever is true, honest, just, pure, lovely
and of good report, think on these things.
Philippians 4: 8

MARILYN MILLER

Joyfully,
Marilyn

Cover Design & Format: DavidMichaelLippman.com

ISBN: 978-1981497072

First Edition

10 9 8 7 6 5 4 3 2 1

DEDICATION

To the many enthusiastic women in my Bible
studies who have encouraged me to keep
writing and teaching

CONTENTS

INTRODUCTION

It all started in 2011 when I was given the opportunity to start an interactive Bible study website for my church. For a whole variety of reasons there are many who cannot attend a study in person so the vision was that this online opportunity would provide a contact with real people as well as motivation and materials to enable them to study the Word of God at their convenience and on their own schedule. This meant that week by week I would be writing a short introduction to each lesson. These intros are what you have in this booklet.

The lingering questions in my mind in the last couple years have been, "Could these brief introductions ever be used in some other way?" Would people find them interesting and inspirational enough to want to read them? Some people who read them through the Facebook group, *We Study Together*, or on the Facebook page, *Women in the Word - We Study Together*, have greatly encouraged me through their comments and insights.

Over the past 16 years I have written more than 30 different Bible study series - some with only 6 lessons and others with up to 14 lessons. Some are book studies while others are topical or word studies. About 20 of them have been formatted for the website - www.westudytogether.com and so they have weekly introductions written for each study.

My thanks go to my daughter, Gretchen Selfridge, for faithfully and carefully finding grammatical errors and refining some of my thoughts and ideas. My friend, Dave Lippman, should receive my appreciation for his expertise and encouragement to make this material into a book. Thanks also to my dear husband, Fred, for patiently and kindly encouraging me to keep on teaching and writing.

May God bless you and enrich your faith and courage in Him as you read and respond to Him.

Marilyn Miller

Thoughts from the series called

LIFE CHANGING PROMISES

A study focused on God's Amazing Promises

By Marilyn Miller for

www.westudytogether.com

EVERYTHING YOU NEED

Have you ever had the experience of answering the phone and hearing some exciting and happy news that is almost unbelievable? Your pulse likely speeds up and a variety of thoughts run through your mind. You might even have to catch your breath because of the deep joy that you feel. Perhaps you've gotten the job you have dreamed of or you're going to get a visit from a dear friend or it is news from the doctor's office that alleviates all your suspicions of an illness. It is at times like this that people often use the phrase, "It's just too good to be true". While the phrase might indicate a skeptical attitude, the reality is that it will take time and trust for you to process the veracity of what you have just been told.

When Jesus told the people that He had come to give them abundant life and to bring the Kingdom of heaven to them, it was news that they could hardly conceive. It probably seemed "too good to be true" to some of them and so they continued to listen, to search, to ask questions, and to wonder. The fact is that many of us continue to do the same thing today. At one level, we nod our heads in agreement when we read the Bible and see the promises that God makes to His children but too often we are tempted to feel that the they are really meant for those who are "more spiritual" than we are or that we do not deserve to receive that kind of mercy or love from Him.

But, guess what! "God never made a promise that is too good to be true." (D. L. Moody) In fact, it is in believing that He really meant what He said that we will be able to have "everything we need for living a Godly life". Sounds almost unbelievable until you, by God's power, step out in faith. It is in trusting His promises that you and I will discover not only who He is but the unlimited riches of His grace and His peace.

Read II Peter 1: 1 - 4

Your thoughts:

Jesus will provide everything I need, not material things, however peace. 3·1·18

THE PROMISE OF PEACE

Did you know that more Americans seek medical treatment for *anxiety* than for back pain or migraine headaches, according to the American Psychological Association? In fact, statistics indicate that the number of people experiencing stress-related physical symptoms, including panic attacks and nervous breakdowns is increasing at an alarming rate. Anxiety, according to the dictionary, "suggests feelings of fear and concern detached from objective sources, feeding themselves, as it were." Living in a rather constant state of uneasiness, unrest, agitation, and anxiousness will often be the root cause for very serious problems in the future.

While our fast-paced American culture with all of our technology and worldwide communication capabilities may aggravate the human tendency to be anxious and worried, it certainly is not a new problem. Jesus knew and understood exactly how His disciples were feeling as He made his destiny known to them. He knew that in addition to understanding how much He loved them, they were going to need His gift of peace. More than once He reassured them that because the Holy Spirit would be with them and in them that they could have peace. In fact, He told them that they would continue to have trials and sorrows while they were here on earth but that IN HIM they could have peace because of His triumph over this world. (John 16: 33)

It's a gift of enormous value. It's a gift that the world cannot give. It's a gift that cost Him dearly. It's a gift that communicates His unlimited love and grace. He is offering it to you!

Read John 14

Your thoughts:

THE PROMISE OF GUIDANCE

If you're thinking about going on a safari in Africa, a dog sledding trip in Alaska, or even river rafting in Colorado, you are probably also hoping that you will have an experienced and knowledgeable guide. Adventures like this take us to new places and usually include physical challenges and stamina beyond our normal experience, so a competent and personable guide will make a huge difference. Ideally you would choose someone who, not only is very knowledgeable and engaging in their conversation, but is also observant, friendly, and flexible. You would also want to have a guide that understands a wise balance between "pushing your boundaries" and safety and who is prepared to make good decisions if there is a crisis or an unexpected challenge. Perhaps, having a guide who you trust and who knows what will be best for you each day of the trip is the one you really want to find.

When it comes to the adventure of life, isn't that what all of us are looking for? While it is easy to pretend, and our culture encourages us to work at independence, the truth is that none of us can see the future or predict when the rapids will be dangerous or where the lions are hiding in the bush. It's one of the reasons that we need God. No other person or belief system can do for us what He can do because He is the only One who offers to us His constant love through His Son, Jesus. He is the only One who has said that He will forgive us when we stray from His path and He will actually guide us by His Holy Spirit and through His Word until we reach our destination. In fact, He will be waiting at heaven's gate to welcome us to "the place that He has prepared for us" when that time comes.

Is there any reason that you wouldn't want to have Him as your guide through life? It's what He has promised to be for all those who "will trust Him and lean not on their own understanding"!

Read Proverbs 3: 1 - 10

Your thoughts:

THE PROMISE OF STRENGTH

Do you have any idea what the synonyms for "inner strength" are in a Thesaurus? Here they are: self-assurance, positive self-image, and aplomb. If that is the kind of fortitude and stability that you are seeking, there are a vast amount of resources available for you - books, classes, articles, counselors, and online materials. No doubt, some of theses ideas will be helpful and empowering, but will they be satisfying and enduring when life is really challenging, the totally unexpected happens, or death is close at hand? It's question that is worth considering quite carefully. Are there other options that you might be wise to explore?

When Paul wrote to his good friends in Philippi, he did give them quite a long list of all of the reasons that he could have felt self-assured and confident in himself and his own efforts. However, none of those things mattered to him compared to the great privilege and joy that he was experiencing in knowing Jesus, his Lord. In fact, he admitted to them that the one and only reason he could be so content, so courageous and so joyful, was that Christ was giving him his strength. He was eager to know "the mighty power that raised Jesus from the dead in his own life". How he longed for his friends to understand and to have this same kind of relationship with Jesus.

Every day, just like the Paul, we have the option to choose SELF-confidence or GOD-confidence. Why is the decision so complicated at times and in certain circumstances? Would it have anything to do with believing God's promises?

Read Philippians 4: 10 - 20

Your thoughts:

THE PROMISE OF GOD'S

FAITHFULNESS

Change is inevitable, isn't it? Sometimes it is welcome and exciting. At other times it is disappointing and painful. It can be a huge stimulus to personal growth and bring new relationships with it or it can bring on times of grief and loss. Often we look forward to and plan our lives around changes that we either want to make or will be coming our way, but it seems that the older one gets, the more often we pass through unexpected times when change descends upon us like a thunder storm. Whatever the changes may feel like to a person, there are always decisions that have to be made and in the process questions that may be difficult to answer.

Perhaps the transitory nature of mankind is exactly the reason that throughout Scripture God reassures His children that He is the changeless One. His love is unending and without limits. His goodness is as trustworthy today as it was in the beginning of time. His faithfulness is new every morning and it always will be. As the writer of Hebrews wrote, "Jesus Christ is the same yesterday, today, and forever." Somehow it is in this reality that you and I can find the courage to face the changes that come into our lives. We can let go of our desire to control things knowing our loving and good and faithful God is not surprised by the events that so easily can overwhelm us. We can find hope and peace in His faithfulness as our Heavenly Father and our Redeemer.

It makes you want to sing, "Great is Your faithfulness, oh, God, my Father. There is no shadow of turning with You. You do not change. Your compassions never fail. As You have been, You forever will be. Great is Your faithfulness, Lord, unto me. Amen!"

Read Lamentations 3: 1 - 42

Your thoughts:

THE PROMISE OF FORGIVENESS

In the words of C.S. Lewis, "We all agree that forgiveness is a beautiful idea until we have to practice it." It is so much easier to talk about it than to really offer it to someone who has hurt or offended us in some way. The tendency is to harbor the resentment, feed the nagging desire for revenge, rationalize or justify our right to be upset, or just to ignore it and hope that the feelings of bitterness will all just go away. In reality, forgiveness is undoubtedly one of the clearest ways to make love visible and to live in the light of God's love.

When God looked through the eyes of His infinite love for mankind, for you and me, and realized that sending His One and Only Son to pay the price for our sin so that He could offer us forgiveness, He didn't hesitate. He didn't spare Jesus the pain and suffering that He experienced. He didn't look for other options. For Him, forgiveness was the only option that absolute love demanded. And "Jesus did not cling to His divine privileges, but willingly humbled Himself and died" in our place so that we could be forgiven, so that we could become children of the living God. (Philippians 2: 6-8) It means that every day we can come into His presence and receive the promise of His forgiveness and the strength to give His love in the same way to others.

Oh the pure joy of willingly, even eagerly, receiving forgiveness from the Lord Jesus so that we can feel free to give to others as we have been given!

Read I John 1: - 2:2

Your thoughts:

THE PROMISE OF A FUTURE
and A HOPE

It has been said "that we can live 40 days without food, 8 days without water, 4 minutes without air, but only a few seconds without hope." What is it about hope that makes it so essential to our lives? Obviously, it is far more than wishful thinking or having an optimistic outlook. The dictionary helps us by defining the idea of hope as "a desire supported by some confidence of its fulfillment". It is an attitude of positive anticipation for what is to come, isn't it? It is what allows us to creatively and enthusiastically look forward to the future.

When you think about some of your favorite heroes in Scripture, you will often read about the hope that they had in God. Abraham found himself in a humanly impossible situation, but "he hoped against hope" that what God promised would really happen. In the Psalms David often expressed that it was his hope in the Lord that enabled him to face danger, disappointment and depression. Reminding himself of God's faithfulness and goodness is what gave him hope. As Jeremiah lamented over the exile of his people and their rebellion against God, he reminded himself "that it is good to hope and quietly wait for the salvation that comes from the Lord". All those who have and continue to put their trust in the "God of Hope" will never be put to shame. That is the reason that the writers of the New Testament epistles could write their letters of encouragement to the believers who were often facing intense persecution and troubles.

What was true for the believers centuries ago, is still true today! God knows all about the plans that He has for us - to give us a future and a hope.

Read Jeremiah 29: 1 - 23

Your thoughts:

THE PROMISE OF

GOD'S TENDER CARE

What mental image comes into your mind when you think about the idea of "tender care"? It may be the picture of a new mother contentedly rocking her little one to sleep or it may be an elderly husband sitting at the bedside of his critically ill wife and gently touching her arm, reassuring her of his love. It might be of someone stirring a very large pot of soup so that the hungry can have a meal or a nurse tending to the wounds of someone who has been injured. It could simply be someone who is willing to take the time to visit and encourage an invalid or make a phone call to a friend who is experiencing grief or loss. Tender care usually comes out of a heart of compassion, doesn't it? The dictionary says that compassion is "the deep feeling of sharing the suffering of another in the inclination to give aid or support, or to show mercy."

One of the phrases that the writers of the Gospels often used as they discussed the way that Jesus lived when He was here on earth was "He was filled with compassion". He saw the multitudes and was moved by their situations. He met individuals and He identified with their pain and their struggles. The sick came to Him to be healed, so He showed them

His mercy and His power in not only healing them physically but offering to them forgiveness of their sins. When the disciples were frightened or hungry, He listened to them and met their needs. Before He left them, He made clear to them that they would not be alone because His Holy Spirit would come to be their advisor and their comforter.   He truly was compassionate.

Did you know that we, too, have Someone who "understands our weaknesses, for He faced all of the same testings we do, yet He did not sin"? In fact, we are told in Hebrews 4: 15 - 16 that "we can come boldly to the throne of our gracious God. There we will receive His mercy and we will find grace to help us when we need it most." That is God's promise to you!

Read I Peter 5: 1 - 14

Your thoughts:

THE PROMISE OF ETERNAL LIFE

Do you remember the old Negro Spiritual, "This World Is Not My Home, I'm Just A'Passing Through"? It was probably written during the earliest days of slavery here in the United States. Undoubtedly, as they sang it in their churches and throughout the day, it reminded them of a place where peace and justice would exist; a place where freedom from bondage would be a reality. It may have given them hope and inspired them to "let their light shine" while they were still on this earth. To sing about their friend, Jesus, and to remind themselves of a better home, their eternal home that was coming soon, would likely have given them hope and brought them joy.

When Jesus came to this world, He often told the crowds that He had come to bring the Kingdom of Heaven to them. While He didn't appear to be the kind of Messiah that they were expecting because he did not come as a political or military leader, His message, His miracles, and His promises were supernatural. Quite often He would tell them that those who would believe in Him would not only be reconciled to God, but they would be given the gift of eternal life. Just before His crucifixion, He explained to them that while He would be leaving them after His resurrection, that they could look forward to the day when He would return and they would be with Him forever. Then they would see the reality of the New Heaven and the New Earth that he promised and live in the light of His presence forever and ever.

Around the world today, believers are still singing a similar refrain in their own languages and among their own people. They might also be singing, "I want to be ready. I want to be ready. Walk in Jerusalem just like John. If you get there before I do, tell all my friends I'm a-coming too." It's the one reality that still brings real comfort and hope.

Read John 3: 1 - 21

Your thoughts:

THE PROMISE OF

ANSWERED PRAYER

Why is it that adults find it so easy to make very simple truths into complex ideas? Could it be a fascination with the ability to use big words or the feeling that long explanations represent wisdom? Whatever the reason, when it comes to some bottom line philosophy, there is one idea that is probably best expressed in its simplest form. A short, but repeated phrase in a well-known children's song says it all. "Yes, Jesus loves me. Yes, Jesus loves me. Yes, Jesus loves me. The Bible tells me so." Because it is at the same time a very basic idea and yet a very complex concept, it is understandable to a young child and yet deeply meaningful to the most educated adult.

When it comes to the subject of prayer, we can talk about the mysteries that surround intercession, supplication, and so much more, but here is the simple truth that will greatly influence how and when you pray. "Yes, Jesus hears me. Yes, Jesus hears me. Yes, Jesus hears me. He loves to answer prayer."

Jesus hears me when I pray.
He delights to hear me say,

"Heavenly Father, I love You,
all because You love me, too.

When the answers are slow to come,
just remember who they're from.
In His time, He'll answer you,
'cause He knows best, it always true.

It's not because you are so good
and you do the things you should.
It's because He loves you so,
His grace and mercy make you grow.

It's in His presence you will find,
His joy and total peace of mind.
He always says, "Please ask some more.
My blessing on you I will pour."

If you ask, I'll give you rest.
My ways are good. They're always best.
He says, "Please trust Me and obey
and I will guide you all the way."

Simple truths and yet so profound!

Read Psalm 145

Your thoughts:

Thoughts from the series called

LIVING BY FAITH

A study of the People of Faith

listed in Hebrews 11

By Marilyn Miller for

www.westudytogether.com

FEAR OR FAITH?

The little girl climbed eagerly up on her father's shoulders. As he walked around In the shallow end of the swimming pool, she felt safe and secure. She laughed and giggled and patted the top of her daddy's head. She watched with glee as he started walking toward the deep end of the pool not realizing that soon the water would creep up to cover his chest and then his shoulders. However it didn't take long before fear began to grip her mind. What if he lost his balance, would she drown? What if the water came up over his head? What if? What if? As her father felt the tightening grip of her hand and realized that there were tears in her eyes, he gently reminded her that she was "as safe in the deep end of the pool as in the shallow end because there was nowhere that he couldn't touch the bottom." There was no time when he would let go of her. Knowing this changed her fears to excitement and her worries to anticipation.

Isn't that little girl a great deal like all of us? When the waters get a little too deep, the waves seem a bit too strong, or the undertow feels like it is going to take us out to sea, we begin to feel afraid. It is so easy to let our imagination start to create situations that lead to anxiety and challenges that seem insurmountable. That is exactly when our Heavenly

Father would like us to hear Him say, "You are as safe in the deep end of the pool as in the shallow end." He would like us to believe that our safety is in His presence and that our hope is as secure as His Word. He would like us to fully trust Him in the complexities and pain of our earthly journey. He would be pleased to share all of His resources with us as we put our faith in Him.

Don't you love knowing that it is Jesus who "initiates and perfects our faith"? (Hebrews12: 2) If this is really true, what's keeping you from letting go of your fears and worries, your complaints and skepticism? What's holding you back from enjoying the ride that He has planned just for you?

Read Hebrews 10: 19 – 11: 3 and 12: 1 - 3

Your thoughts:

AUTHENTIC?

Authentic could be considered a buzzword these days. We want to know that the products we buy are the quality and kind that we desire to purchase. When you are paying top dollar, it is important to know whether the Rolex watch is real or fake. Is the leather in the purse or briefcase genuine or synthetic? While this kind of information is practical, when the word is used to describe your boss, your teacher, and even your friend, it takes on a new depth of importance. You want to know that the people who are most important in your life, who can influence your present and your future success, are trustworthy, predictable and real. You want to know that what they say and do reflects who they really are so that there will be consistency and credibility in your relationship to them.

What does it take to be *authentic* would you say? Looking at the old, old story in Genesis of Cain and Abel might give you some important clues. They each brought gifts to the Lord - one was from the harvest of his fields and the other was from his flock of lambs. One was accepted and one was rejected. Why? What did Abel do that Cain did not do? What did Abel understand that Cain missed out on? What important clues can be found in God's conversation with Cain? What attitudes and actions help you to

26

get a glimpse of the motives behind the gifts? Was God looking more for external performance or internal authenticity?

Simply said, it could be that long before Abraham obeyed God or Moses wrote the ten commandments, God had placed in the heart of man the desire to love Him and to offer up the best that we have of ourselves and our possessions to Him. The truth is that since sin came into the world, everyone has the choice to listen to the quiet call of God in humility or submission or to try to figure out life without Him. It may be the difference between those two brothers. What do you think?

Read Hebrews 11: 4 and Genesis 4: 1 - 16

Your thoughts:

THE JOY OF GIFT GIVING

Do you like giving gifts? They can be gifts that you purchase or presents that cost you time, thought and/or energy rather than money. They can be wrapped with beautiful paper and ribbons or wrapped with thoughtfulness and affection for someone. We give gifts to express our love and admiration or perhaps our gratefulness or concern for other people. In choosing a gift, the motive behind it is usually to find a way to please them, to bring them a smile or to make them feel cherished or appreciated. Sometimes gifts express sentiments and love in a way that words cannot adequately do. When you give a gift that you know has greatly pleased the recipient, not only is he/she extremely happy, but so are you. Right?

When we read the very brief biography of Enoch, it is interesting to take note of the reason that he is included in this list of heroes of faith in Hebrews. We are told that "he pleased God" - he gave God clear evidence of his love by doing the things that brought Him joy. Many centuries later the way that God showed us His love was through giving. "For God so loved the world that He gave . . . " - John 3: 16. Our desire to love and to be loved is made clearly visible through all kinds of gift-giving, isn't it? Surprisingly this is not limited to only our human relationships, but is also demonstrated in the way we choose to live a life that is pleasing to God. Do you agree that the gift that brings Him the greatest joy is our willingness to believe and to keep on trusting Him - every hour of every day?

The song says, "All to Jesus I Surrender. All to Him I freely give. I will ever love and trust Him and in His presence daily live. I surrender all. I surrender all. All to Thee my blessed Savior, I surrender all." That just might be the ultimate gift that we can give to the Lord. What do you think?

Read Hebrews 11: 5 - 6 and Genesis 5: 18 - 24

Your thoughts:

WALKING TOGETHER

There is just something that is so pleasant about taking a walk with a good friend. Good conversation often accompanies the unhurried steps but you can also have long pauses of silence, simply enjoying the scenery that surrounds you. Unconsciously you may even walk in step with your companion. Walking together does mean some rather obvious decisions, however. You need to be headed in the same direction. Both of you must at least tacitly agree on the pace at which you will go. It might mean that one of you must slow down or speed up so that you can comfortably stay side by side. Walking together gives both of you the assurance that you are not alone, that someone wants to spend time with you, and that together you may make some discoveries that will bring solace or joy or hope or new insight to each of you.

Isn't it interesting that in the biography that we have of Noah in the book of Genesis, it is recorded that he "walked with God"? In fact, one translation even says that "he walked in close fellowship with God". While it is a phrase that is used throughout the Bible, it is not often used to describe a specific person. Moses recommended throughout the Pentateuch that the Israelites should "walk after the Lord their God" or that they should "walk in all His ways". The prophet Micah reminded them that "it is good to do right, to love mercy, and to walk humbly with your God." Perhaps it was on one of their walks together that God told Noah His plan for him to build a big ark so that his family and the animals would be safe when the big storm came. Perhaps it was on those regular walks that Noah responded to God and then did all that God commanded him to do. Certainly as he walked around the ark with God, he knew in amazing ways that God would surely keep His promises.

Wouldn't you like to be remembered as someone who not only walked with God but lived "by faith in the Son of God"? As someone who actually stayed in step with Him?

Read Hebrews 11: 7 and Genesis 6 - 9:3

Your thoughts:

WAITING, WAITING, WAITING

How do you react when you are told that you will have to wait longer than you expected for an appointment? Or when you discover that the traffic is at a standstill on the freeway? Or that your flight has been delayed for several hours meaning that you will undoubtedly miss your connecting flight? The natural tendency is to have increased anxiety and to wonder how these delays will affect all of your plans. For some people these times can mean an increase in their blood pressure. As the seed thoughts of worry and fear start to grow, waiting can even make some people respond to life with outbursts of frustration and anger. The questions of "why?" or "why me?" can sometimes override the desire for patience and the willingness to look to God for peace.

An even greater challenge for those of us who desire to "live by faith" is waiting on God to do the things that He has promised to do for us in His Word. No Old Testament hero occupies more focus in the New Testament than Abraham. Perhaps it is because Abraham learned both through failure and success that God's ways were far superior to his own plans. He learned that it was always best to listen to God and to follow Him even when the destination was not clear. He discovered that God would definitely keep

His promises, but that His timetable might be very different than he had anticipated. When his biggest test came, Abraham's faith was strong enough to believe "Yahweh-Yireh" (the LORD will provide") and that He would still "bless him and multiply his descendants beyond number." He was willing to "wait on the LORD".

How do you respond when it feels like God is asking you to do something that seems impossible? What helps you when God asks you to wait for His timing and for His direction? Where do you find hope? How do you keep your eyes on God's promise of eternal life with Him?

Read Hebrews 11: 8 – 19

and Genesis 17: 1 – 16 and 21: 1 – 8

Your thoughts:

HOW WILL YOU BE DESCRIBED?

What do you remember about your mom or dad that makes you smile? What did they do right? In what ways did they pass on to you values and beliefs that have given you strength or courage or confidence? Perhaps it is not your parents that you turn to when you think in positive terms about the things that were handed down to you from your past. It may be your grandparents or even other adults who played a significant role in your formative years. The legacy that we all leave for those who follow in our footsteps is far more than money, property, or heirlooms. It is primarily about "leaving what you learned more than what you earned." It is the transferring of what we hold most dear from one generation to the next and in doing so giving them both a blessing and hope for the future.

Who would have guessed that the legacy of a life of obedient faith that Abraham passed on to Isaac would be remembered for centuries? Who would have believed that the more quiet and consistent life of faith of Isaac would be recorded for posterity? Who would have known that the blessings and predictions that Jacob gave to his sons would stand as an example for untold generations to come? Who would have predicted that Joseph's incredible understanding and acceptance by faith of God's sovereign will would become a legacy by which people today could find encouragement and renewal of their own faith?

As you think about the legacy that you are now creating, what are the words which will be used to describe you, the values by which you will be remembered, the reasons that your memory will be treasured?

Read Hebrews 11: 20 - 22

Your thoughts:

MAKING DECISIONS

How many decisions do you make in a day? Some internet sources estimate that an adult makes about "35,000 remotely conscious ones" every day. Of course, most of those decisions are made by our fast and intuitive mind, so that they barely register as a choice. From our earliest morning moments to the final minutes before we drift off to sleep we have the privilege and power to make decisions. The great majority of them seem to have very little impact on our destiny or our future, but there are some that have long-lasting consequences. Why is it that some people seem to make such wise choices while others seem to never learn from their experience and mistakes? What advice would you give to help others learn to do a better job of weighing the facts and options so that they can make timely and wise decisions?

When it comes to finding a Biblical hero that can give us very practical advice on how to make good choices, you might want to look to Moses. Isn't it interesting that when the temptation came for him to stay and enjoy a life of privilege and prestige, he chose to return to his own suffering people? Why? When God appeared to him and gave him a very intense and dangerous job to do, he listened and obeyed. Why? After he led the Israelites through the

Red Sea, the first thing he did was to lead the people in a song of praise and adoration because of what the LORD had done for them. Why? While Moses did pay the consequences of some poor choices, we remember him most for the ways in which he deliberately chose to believe God's promises. Some day the Israelites would live in a "land flowing with milk and honey". In the meantime, Moses stepped out BY FAITH to do the things that God wanted to accomplish through him. It wasn't easy, was it? But, he kept right on going because he kept his eyes on "the one who is invisible." It was all BY FAITH.

Where do you keep your eyes when it is time to make those big decisions? Where is your focus when you face a challenge or are given a new opportunity to trust in Yahweh - the great I AM?

Read Hebrews 11: 23 - 29

Your thoughts:

FACING OUR FEARS AND DOUBTS

Do you think that "living by faith" means that there is a total absence of fear or anxiety? Does it mean that you have complete and unwavering trust in God? Does it mean that you cannot allow yourself to doubt and that you must deny any questions that seem to creep into your mind unbeckoned? Is it something that God willingly gives to all His children or is it a gift that they receive in varying amounts? You could spend hours discussing these kinds of questions with others who also embrace whole- heartedly the fact that it is "by faith that we are saved" and it is "by faith we continue to experience the life that we have in Christ". The fact remains that honesty demands that all of us admit that faith does not eradicate completely our fears, our doubts or our questions. In fact, it just might be that these are the very things that cause us to learn what it means to take a new step of faith - "the willingness to let what we believe determine our actions."

One of the most unlikely women of faith in the Bible was not an Israelite. She was a woman with a questionable background. She lived in a very strategic place in Jericho at a very crucial time in history. She had the same fears that her family and neighbors had. She had heard about the power and intentions of the Israelites to come and destroy them completely. BUT, unlike the people in her city who refused to acknowledge the supreme God, she turned her heart and loyalties to Him. She was willing to take some big risks and trust that this God would protect her and her family. She did not let fear dominate her decisions. She did not let her past reputation limit her future or her concerns diminish her willingness to do something courageous. Little did she know, that in choosing to trust God at a time when she really had to stand alone, how He would bless her so greatly in the future.

Do you have some fears? Some doubts? Some questions? Perhaps it is time to look more at the God of history and let His Holy Spirit capture your imagination and your mind in a new way. He's waiting and willing. Are you?

Read Hebrews 11: 30 - 31, Joshua 2: 1 - 24
and 5: 10 - 6: 27

Your thoughts:

"FAITH-FULL"

When is the last time that you read a really great biography of someone who lived an exemplary life of faith in God? Individuals who were able to live courageously and joyfully in spite of real hardship and persecution? People who were called by God to stand up for their beliefs, to share the Gospel in foreign cultures, to speak out against evil and corruption, or to walk through hostile doors in order to defend the truth? Maybe you have read the story of Dietrich Bonhoeffer, Billy Graham, Jim or Elizabeth Elliot, or Mother Teresa. Perhaps you have read about Amy Carmichael, William Wilberforce, George Muller, Brother Andrew, Martin Luther, Hudson Taylor or St. Augustine. Throughout the centuries, there have always been those people who chose to listen to God and to step out by faith to do the things that He had prepared for them to accomplish. Their stories continue to bring new courage and inspiration to everyone who reads them.

Isn't it interesting that the writer of Hebrews singled out only a few examples of people who lived "by faith" so long ago but clearly realized that there are multitudes of other "unsung heroes" who really could have been included? Apparently the one thing that all of them had in common was that they truly believed that God would keep His promises. For them, this meant the coming of the Messiah - the One who would liberate them and set them free from the tyranny of oppression and bondage. The One who would bring peace and security for the people of God. The One that the prophets said would reign forever. Counting on this, they were willing to endure whatever temporary difficulties that came into their lives. They were committed to remain "Faith-Full."

"Dear friends, we are already God's children but He has not yet shown us what we will be like when Christ appears. But we do know that we will be like Him, for we will see Him as He really is. And all who have this eager expectation will keep themselves pure, just as He is pure." (I John 3: 2 - 3)   When your biography is written, will people say that this is what kept you going?

Read Hebrews 11: 32 - 40

Your thoughts:

YOUR THEME SONG

Although she knows the words and melody for at least 25 songs, her theme song this morning is "Jesus Loves Me, This I Know." Two weeks ago when she visited me, it was, "Oh, How I Love Jesus." She sang these songs as she built with blocks and rocked the teddy bear. She sang them while she sat in the big recliner chair to look at her books and as she waited for the next little pancake. She sang them as we walked down the road and she picked up the small pinecones, a few little rocks and then some leaves. When her pockets got too full, she told me her treasures were too heavy and we dumped them out so that she could start again. She sang them as she stopped to watch the squirrels and listen to the birds and even when she tripped and fell off the little ledge she was walking on. She is just 2 years old and already has some favorite songs.

When the Bible encourages us to praise the Lord and to worship Him, is there any better way to do that than to use the vehicle of song and of music? Whether you prefer the Psalms, the old hymns of the church, or the newer expressions of praise music that have been written, they all provide wonderful options for "keeping your eyes on Jesus". What better way to help us draw our minds from the visible to the invisible than to sing "Great is Your

Faithfulness" or to focus on a prayer like, "Guide Me, Oh Thou Great Jehovah"? Or how about "Great is Our God" or "He is Mighty to Save"? What better way to remind ourselves throughout the day and in the night time hours that we have a God who knows us, who loves us, and who came to our world so that we might have life through His name?

Like my little friend, why not start each day with a song? What one would you choose for today? Maybe it should simply be, "Jesus loves me, this

I know - for the Bible tells me so."

Read Hebrews 12: 1 - 13
and Romans 5: 1 - 11

Your thoughts:

Thoughts from the series called

BECAUSE OF HIS GREAT LOVE

A study focused on Paul's Letter

to the Ephesians

By Marilyn Miller for

www.westudytogether.com

HOW RICH ARE YOU?

What is it that makes someone feel that he or she is rich? Is it the size of their bank account or their investments? Is it their possessions or their positions or their sense of entitlement? Or could it be that it is simply how they view life? One research center claims that 54% of Americans define rich people as "anyone who simply makes money more than they do." It seems so obvious that the amount of wealth which one accumulates or inherits has little to do with being really and truly rich. In fact, playing the "comparison game" is a sure way to convince yourself that you are a loser in life because there will always be others who have more of whatever it is that you want.

When Paul wrote his letter to the believers in Ephesus, he earnestly desired that they understand how blessed, how rich, they were because of their new relationship to God. In fact, he seems quite excited about reminding them that "in Christ" they had EVERY spiritual blessing. After all, they had been chosen, predestined, redeemed, and forgiven through Him. If only they could really grasp what this meant in a deeper way, it would totally have changed their outlook on life, wouldn't it? If you knew that while you can only have part of your inheritance right now but that your full inheritance was guaranteed for the future, it would totally impact your thinking about how blessed, how "wealthy" you really are.

Do you want to feel that you are richer than your present material circumstances would indicate? It just might be that Paul's prayer for his friends would point you in the right direction. "Shine your light on the hope You are calling them to embrace. Reveal to them the glorious riches You are preparing as their inheritance. Let them see the full extent of Your power that is at work in those who believe." (Ephesians 1:18 - 19 - The Voice)

Read Ephesians 1

Your thoughts:

EXTRAVAGENT MERCY

What comes to your mind when you think of the idea of mercy? A judge? A teacher? A parent? A humanitarian or philanthropist? Webster's dictionary says that mercy is "the kind or forgiving treatment of someone who could be treated harshly. It is kindness or help given to people who are in a very bad or desperate situation." Almost every religion holds it up as an attribute that is not only desirable but characteristic of people who want to please their deity. When it is within the power or right of someone to punish another, to give them what they deserve according to the law or their own standards, or to even to harm someone else, the response can only be a call for mercy and compassion, for leniency or even forgiveness.

When we read in Ephesians that God is RICH IN MERCY, it should not be a surprise to us. Even the Old Testament heroes, like Abraham, Moses and David saw God as totally merciful. The prophets told the Israelites that a Savior would come some day to rescue them from their pain and suffering solely because of His compassion. John the Baptist proclaimed that in God's mercy, He had sent His son to be "the lamb of God who would take away the sin of the world." (John 1: 29) God's willingness to "forgive and to make us alive in Christ" gives us a whole new dimension to the concept of mercy, doesn't it? It's what we call justification. We don't deserve it. We can't earn it. But "through faith we are justified and have peace with God through our Lord Jesus Christ." (Romans 4: 1l) That's what extravagant mercy is!

Thank you, God, that in Your grace "You give us what we do not deserve" and in Your mercy "You do not give us what we really and truly do deserve." Thank You that Your mercy extends to all generations, to all people, and to everyone, everywhere.

Read Ephesians 2

Your thoughts:

CHOOSING ADOPTION

Why do people choose to adopt a child? Probably the most common reason is that a couple finds they can't have one of their own, so adoption becomes the sole means by which they can have the joy of parenting. Others adopt children because they want to provide a safe and loving environment for little ones who do not have a home. Why would someone choose to adopt a child with special needs or disabilities?" Why would they open up their hearts to a little one who will never be able to do the things that a normal child might do and will probably end up costing them a great deal of time and energy for their entire lifetime? Is it a great capacity to love and care for a single human being that ultimately is the reason that they are willing to make a permanent space in their hearts and home for an unloved or needy child?

The Good News that Paul shares with these believers is that God, from the beginning of time, had a plan in place to adopt as His children all those who would by faith come to Him. In fact, He promised to Abraham that not only the Jews, but that all nations would someday be blessed through him and his descendants. As it says in Galatians 4, "When the right time came, God sent His Son . . . to buy freedom for us who were slaves to the law, so that He could adopt us as His very own children . . . and

His heirs." Why would God want to adopt a disabled, needy and sinful person into His family? Over and over again, the Bible tells us that it was because of His great love for us. Love so great that He reached down to us to make us a new creation through His Spirit so that we could become His heirs and live in His presence now and throughout eternity.

"May you experience the love of Christ, though it is too great to understand fully. Then you will be made complete with all the fullness of life and power that comes from God." (Ephesians 3: 19 - NLT) It's Paul's prayer for the people that he loved. May it be my prayer and yours, as well.

Read Ephesians 3

Your thoughts:

EXTREME MAKEOVER

Did you ever watch the TV program "Extreme Makeover"? It's absolutely surprising what a crew of planners and professionals can do to totally renovate a home and garden in one week. They race against the clock in order to remodel or reconstruct every room in the house so that a deserving family will have a home that is like new. The surprise on the owners' faces and the joy in their hearts seems to sufficiently reward those who have worked so hard to accomplish all of the necessary tasks that are involved in changing the rather pathetic place to a desirable home.

Have you ever compared this kind of total renovation to your own need for transformation? Paul explains this in his letter like this: "Put off your old sinful nature and your former way of life, which is corrupted by lust and deception. Put on your new nature, created to be like God - truly righteous and holy." It's not a job that those believers could ever accomplish by themselves, is it? There isn't any way that any of them would have the expertise, the dedication, or the ability to change their behavior in such a dramatic way. It's not a job that you or I can tackle on our own either. The good news is that God knew all this about us and so He not only sent Jesus, but He sent the Holy Spirit, who is waiting and able to renew our thoughts and attitudes. Through His power, we can experience a radical change in our choices and behavior. Does it mean that the job will be completed in a day or a week or even a year? Obviously not. It is a change that generally occurs step by step, throughout a whole lifetime, as we trust in Him.

.

There is no lottery or application for this kind of personal extreme makeover, is there? All that is required is a humble heart and grateful spirit. Is it what you really want God to do for you?

Read Ephesians 4

Your thoughts:

WHO LIKES SUBMISSION?

Would you agree that some children just seem to be born with a very strong will? They're determined to have their own way no matter the cost. Many books have been written to help the parents of "strong-willed, spirited or powerful" children. While they may be enormously challenging as they are growing up, the good news is that they often make terrific and very productive adults because they are willing to stand up for what they believe and to tenaciously work to accomplish their goals. On the down side of that kind of personality can be an unwillingness to cooperate or to even listen to the ideas and suggestions of other people unless they learn to combine a humble and teachable spirit with their determined ways.

When Paul explains to the believers in his letter what it means to be "filled with the Spirit", guess what he includes in his list? It looks like this, "speak psalms and sing spiritual songs with others, make music in your own heart, give thanks for everything and submit to one another out of reverence for Christ." Why would the idea of submission be included in this list do you suppose? Could it be that a spirit of real worship and heartfelt gratefulness to the Lord Jesus always leads to a deep desire to honor Him through the way that we respond tp the people in our lives, especially those that are closest to you? If one is really anxious to be wise and to please the Lord, Paul makes it quite clear that this will mean that the commandment which was given so long ago is still important - "Love your neighbor as yourself" or said in another way, "Be willing to honor God by looking not only at your own interests (and desires) but at the interests of others". (Philippians 2: 4)

Would you describe yourself as strong willed? Thank God for it because it can help you greatly as you take seriously the opportunity to live life first of all in submission to the Lord. The prayer of Jesus to His Father in the garden just before He was betrayed and arrested is a great place to start every day, "I want Your will to be done, not mine." It can make submission to others a joyous reality.

Read Ephesians 5: 1 - 6: 9

Your thoughts:

READY or NOT?

If only we knew when the earthquake was coming, the burglar would arrive, the accident would happen, the financial crisis would begin, or the heart attack would strike, we could be so much better prepared. We could gather in our supplies, buy the right kind of insurance, avoid going to certain places, keep our money under the mattress, or eat more wisely and exercise more. However, that is simply not the way life works, is it? In the physical and material realm of life, we never know what a day will bring and so we do our best to be wise and to be prepared for emergencies, knowing that there is a balance between caution and passivity, imagination and reality. We can work at "staying calm and carrying on."

In the arena of spiritual battles, it is a very different story. We know that the devil and his spiritual cohorts are eager to find ways to make life difficult, to discourage, or to bring disaster on those who follow the Lord. From Genesis to Revelation God helps us to understand the reality of the "enemy" as well as some of his varied tactics and unpredictable ways of attacking God's people. Perhaps that is why Paul, at the end of his letter to the Ephesians, once again reminded his dear friends that there was a way to stay strong, to keep on winning the skirmishes as well as the battles that were bound to come to each of them in unpredictable ways throughout life. There is a way to be prepared to meet temptation and to even help our friends be successful in their battles.

It might be a very good idea for you to check your "armor" right now! Is it readily available? Is there a piece that is missing or broken? And finally, are you really alert and listening to your "commander"?

Read Ephesians 6: 10 - 24

Your thoughts:

Thoughts from the series called

THE QUESTIONS
JESUS ASKED

A study of the Gospel written by Mark

By Marilyn Miller for

www.westudytogether.com

WHAT IS ON YOUR SCHEDULE?

How do you decide what to do each day? For many, because of work or school or other commitments, there are only a few precious hours during the day when you have the luxury of deciding how you will spend that time.   For others there is a greater opportunity to make choices for many hours every day. Rich Warren in his book, <u>The Purpose-Driven Life</u>, reminds us, "Time is your most precious gift because you only have a set amount of it. You can make more money, but you can't make more time. When you give someone your time, you are giving them a portion of your life that you'll never get back. Your time is your life. That is why the greatest gift you can give someone is your time."

When Jesus started his 3-year public ministry, it is clear that He knew from the beginning that every day was an important day to accomplish his mission. In the Gospel written by Mark, we quickly discover the urgency and dedication that Jesus had to make sure that He lived out His purpose and His passion. One of the fascinating observations that you might want to make is the number of times Mark uses the phrases such as "at once", "without delay, and "immediately". Yet Jesus never seemed to be in a hurry. He always had time for individuals in need, for responding to His critics, and for preaching and teaching the people. He also had energy to get up early so that He could be by Himself to pray. As you read the first two chapters in Mark this week, why don't you take note of the things that were most important to Jesus. What were the guidelines that Jesus used to help Him decide how to spend His time? What did He want to accomplish day by day so that the people would begin to understand that He was indeed the Son of God and the Son of Man?

In a world of distractions, interruptions, delays, and unlimited choices, what keeps you on track? How do your goals and your deepest desires impact the way that you spend your hours and minutes each day?

Read Mark 1: 9 - 45

Your thoughts:

WHAT IS A MIRACLE?

What would you say is a "miracle" is? Is it simply something that happened that was unexpected or a big surprise, something that you didn't think would be possible or causes you to stand in awe and wonder? The dictionary says a miracle is "an event that appears unexplainable by the laws of nature and so is held to be supernatural in origin or an act of God." Another way of looking at a miracle is that it is the intervention of God in the normal course of nature at exactly the right moment in order to accomplish His purposes or to display His own power and glory.

How many miracles do you think that Mark described in his short Gospel? He was focused in his action packed writing to make sure that the readers would grasp that Jesus had power and authority over nature, disease, death and evil. He wanted the Romans to see and know Jesus for who He really was. As one reads about these miracles which drew crowds of people to Jesus wherever He went, you realize that they also threatened the established leaders of the Jewish community. Rather than stand in amazement and respond with curiosity and sincere questions, they responded defensively with hostility and jealousy. Did that stop Jesus? Did it cause Him to respond with aggression? As you look at Mark 3, it is clear that while Jesus certainly felt deeply about his opponents, He also carefully posed questions, told stories and always spoke truthfully to them in order to make His identity and mission clear.

Do you believe that Jesus' is still doing miracles today? I do. As the songwriter so beautifully expressed it, "It took a miracle to put the stars in place. It took a miracle to hang the world in space. But when He saved my soul, cleansed and made me whole, it took a miracle of love and grace." Keep your eyes open. Keep your mind alert. God is still at work accomplishing His purposes and displaying His power and glory - often when you least expect it.

Read Mark 2: 1 - 12

Your thoughts:

STORIES WITH A PURPOSE

There is no question that storytelling, while one of the most ancient art forms, is still one of the greatest and most effective means of communication. Stories capture the attention of people in all stages of life. In fact someone has said, "After nourishment, shelter and companionship, stories are the thing we need most in this world." Stories help us to process life, to use our imaginations, and to share in experiences that we could never have on our own. From the classroom to the boardroom, from the homeless shelter to the mansion, well-told stories have the power to change both hearts and minds.

Perhaps these are just a few of the reasons that Jesus often communicated through simple stories that we call parables. He wanted His listeners to begin to understand and visualize what the Kingdom of Heaven was really like and to grasp spiritual realities in concrete ways. As the disciples, crowds, and Jewish leaders listened to Jesus' parables, the meaning of them was often not obvious, so Jesus would spend time explaining them to His disciples and those "who had ears to hear". When we read these same parables centuries later, we, too, need to listen with open ears and minds to the things that the Holy Spirit would teach us through them. Keeping in mind the setting in which Jesus told the parable and looking at the heart of the story rather than every little detail often helps us begin to grasp the point or truth that is being illustrated. As Jesus often said to those were teachable, "Consider carefully what you hear!"

Some things do not ever change. There is still a big continuum of response to this man called Jesus and to the stories that He told, isn't there? From antagonist to supporter, from doubter to believer, from curious to self-satisfied, from open-minded to totally closed. Where would you say you are on this spectrum?

Read Mark 4: 1 - 20

Your thoughts:

WHAT IS COMPASSION?

Remember Winnie the Pooh and his friend Eeyore? One day Pooh Bear was walking along the riverbank and noticed that Eeyore, his stuffed donkey friend, was floating downstream on his back and obviously troubled about the possibility that he might drown. So Pooh asked Eeyore if he had fallen in. Eeyore, trying to appear to be in complete control simply said, "Silly of me, wasn't it?" Apparently Pooh felt that this was the time for a little advice so he recommended to his friend that he be more careful next time. It was then that Pooh looked with a little further concern and noticed that his friend might actually be sinking, but it still did not move him to action. Finally, in desperation, Eeyore actually asked Pooh to rescue him, which, of course, Pooh gladly did. Still, in his nonchalant way of living, Pooh said, "Next time ask me a little sooner". You might conclude that while Pooh in this particular story had sincere sympathy and concern, he did not have compassion.

While compassion is really a noun, it also implies the willingness to act - to actually "be compassionate". When Mark expressed the reason that Jesus healed the demon-possessed man, he said that it was because of His compassion. When he described the scene on the hillside where the hungry crowds had gathered, He told the readers that it was Jesus' heartfelt compassion that caused Him to perform an amazing miracle so that everyone could have something to eat. Jesus might have felt pity, and sometimes sorrow, for the people He met. However, He never stopped there. He always reached out in mercy and compassion, didn't He? He continuously demonstrated for His followers what it looks like to serve, to love and to have mercy.

Why is it that, just like our imaginary friend, Winnie the Pooh, we are so prone to politely and even sympathetically watch a struggling friend, when actually we could really do something to help them or even rescue them? No one is asking us to solve the world's problems but getting out of our easy chair to show compassion to someone today might be worth considering.

Read Mark 6: 30 - 44

Your thoughts:

IT'S HOW YOU SAY IT

Do you remember the age-old adage, "It's not what you say, but how you said it that really matters"? Researchers agree that somewhere between 35 and 40% of our communication is not through the words that we use but through the tone, inflection and speed of our voices. Every child knows the difference between hearing his/her name called affectionately and hearing it spoken when his/her father's patience has come to an end. Intuitively we all listen for the pauses, the words that are emphasized and the intensity of the speaker's voice. The feelings and emotions that are conveyed through our voices influences greatly how the listener interprets the words. Would you agree that the volume, or lack or it, also either enhances the preciseness of the thoughts that are being spoken or may even totally distract from the desired intent?

It is fascinating to consider the kind of voice that Jesus may have used when He was talking to the Pharisees and teachers of the law. Was it a voice that conveyed pity or a touch of anger or frustration or something else? How did his words sound when He was responding to the women with the demon-possessed child or the mute man or the blind man? Even more personally, have you considered what it might have been like to hear Jesus talk about His own future, about the fact that He knew He would be killed and would rise again in 3 days? Was it a pensive and thoughtful announcement? The only clue that Scripture gives us is that He spoke plainly or openly to both His disciples and the crowd that was there. What was His tone of voice when he rebuked Peter and then went on to tell them what it would mean if they were serious about following Him? What was it like for the disciples to hear Him describe what it would mean to follow Him in the days ahead?

There is no doubt that the way that we "hear" His voice today greatly impacts our response. How carefully do you "listen" to the words that you read in your Bible?

Read Mark 7: 1 -23

Your thoughts:

MORE THAN ADVICE

In a world where we are bombarded with all kinds of advice, how do you choose what to take seriously? Do this. Eat that. Buy this. Come here. Go there. There are 3 major reasons that people will begin to listen to the counsel and advice that others give to them. The first is driven by a personal need to hear it because of being aware of a reason why this information would help them solve a problem or answer a question that they have. The second consideration is based on the authority, experience, and trustworthiness of the one giving the advice. Finally, people are more prone to heed the advice of others when they know what the motivation really is for giving it to them.

When Jesus began His public ministry, he invited 12 ordinary men to follow Him. Their "internship" would take them to many cities and expose them to all kinds of people, needs, and situations. As they witnessed His miracles, listened to Him teach, and spent personal time with Him, they were exposed to a new way of looking at life, responding to people, and thinking about the future. When Jesus talked to them and to the crowds, He was a master at giving them far more than good advice, He wove in through illustrations, questions, and admonition, principles and guidance that would serve not only them, but believers throughout the ages and in every culture. Sometimes His advice was surprising. While it was not always easy to hear, it was always consistent with His behavior and life. Jesus always made it clear that for His followers, there was never a choice whether to ignore or not. It was always to become the new way to live your life.

How good are you at following advice? Not just any counsel or promotion that you hear, but the "advice" that Jesus, the Son of God, has left for us in His Word.

Read Mark 9: 33: 50

Your thoughts:

THE PATH TO GREATNESS

Experts tell us that the sense of "entitlement" is a growing phenomenon in our culture. It is defined as a "feeling or belief that you deserve to be given something simply because of who you are." It could be in the form of compensation, special privileges and rights, recognition, or even power. Throughout history most of these assets were given or awarded to someone because of their hard work, willingness to sacrifice, and their desire to take responsibility seriously and conscientiously. Parents have always wanted to provide a better and sometimes an easier life for their children than they experienced but it would seem that in more recent history this has often been at the expense of teaching the next generation the enormous value of needing to earn what you receive and to think as much about the needs of others as your own needs and desires. Would you agree that "entitlement" is one of the greatest enemies of "servanthood"?

When Jesus responded to 2 of His disciples who came to Him asking for the privilege of sitting next to Him in His kingdom, He clearly understood that they were feeling that they somehow deserved those seats of prominence. Since they still believed that the Kingdom of Heaven would soon be established, they obviously wanted to be sure that they would be right beside Him. Isn't it interesting that Jesus did not point out to them their selfishness or become indignant with them for asking the question? Instead, he responded with a question, some direct information, and a personal example of what being the greatest looks like for those who are willing to follow Him. Because He, "being in very nature God, did not consider equality with God something to be grasped, but made Himself nothing taking the very nature of a servant, being made in human likeness", could with absolute integrity demonstrate the path to greatness. (Philippians 2:6 - 7)

A good test might be to look more carefully at how you respond when someone treats you or sees you as a servant rather than at your deeds of service.

Read Mark 10: 35 - 45

Your thoughts:

WHAT'S NEXT?

What is the question that people ask both themselves and others at the completion of any major event? It might at the time of a graduation, at the end of an assignment with the military, or even when you get home from a wonderful vacation. It could be after an unexpected reversal in finances or the loss of a loved one. As people look forward to the next step in their career or family, what they want to know is "what's next?" What are the things that you are looking forward to doing? What are your plans and goals? Where do you think you will be in the coming months? Both our immediate and long-range futures are a big part of how we experience the present. Knowing what might be next influences the choices that we make today.

As the 2 disciples followed Jesus' instruction to go into the next village and get a colt that no one had ever ridden before, they must have wondered what would be next. Little did any of His disciples understand that in a short time the crowds would gather and there would be a wonderful celebration of the One who could do amazing miracles and who could speak with authority about so many things. As they walked with Jesus down the road toward the temple in Jerusalem, listening to the voices of the people shouting, "Hosanna - Save Us" and "Blessed is He who comes in the name of the Lord", they might have started to believe that the Messiah would indeed set up His kingdom in the immediate future or they might have felt totally confused and concerned. What did Jesus mean when He said that He must die and rise again? What would really happen now that they were back in Jerusalem and both the chief priests and the teachers of the law were trying to kill Jesus? They knew that Jesus was certainly in charge of His destiny but what was the next thing on His agenda?

When you find yourself asking the question, "what's next, Lord", it's a great time to remind yourself that while things may look uncertain and confusing, Jesus always invites you to keep walking with Him because He knows the future and understands your fears and your concerns. He has promised to take care of YOU!

Read Mark 11: 1 - 13 and Mark 11: 27 - 33

Your thoughts:

WHAT DOES ARGUING
ACCOMPLISH?

Have you ever known someone who seems to love to argue just for the sake of arguing? Perhaps he or she simply wants to stimulate conversation, discover new ideas or to uncover truth. More often, however, arguments are much more emotionally based. They are driven by the need to be right or in control or the desire to win or feel superior in some way. Someone has wisely said, "If you're arguing with someone for more than 5 minutes, chances are it's not about them or even about the subject matter, but it's about you." Arguments can also be driven by the need to put others in a poorer light than your self or even to purposefully cause the other person to feel threatened or to look bad. In some cases, an argument is the defensive mechanism that is used whenever that individual feels threatened or needs to blame someone else for a problem or crisis.

As the antagonism, frustration, and anger in the hearts and minds of the Pharisees, Sadducees and teachers of the law increased, they often came to Jesus to try to catch Him with theological questions. They probably would have loved to spend time arguing with Him in front of the people, in the hopes that they could put Him in a negative light or prove to the listeners that they were right and righteous and that Jesus was uninformed and a sinner. The amazing thing about Jesus' responses was that He never needed to satisfy their argumentative schemes because He was able to turn their trick questions or leading comments into an opportunity to explain truth and sometimes to point out quite directly the errors in their thinking. When one teacher did respond in a positive and open way to an answer that Jesus gave to Him, He was very quick to encourage that man's wisdom. It wasn't ever about winning or losing for Jesus, it was only about doing the things that His Father had sent Him to do.

Can you think of a time when arguing was a really good idea? Can you recall a time when both parties were winners?

Read Mark 12: 13 - 34

Your thoughts:

WHAT'S ON YOUR LIST?

Do you like to make lists? Things you need to do today. E-mails you need to write or phone calls you really should make. Groceries that you want to buy the next time you are at Costco or Trader Joes. House projects you want to accomplish. Whether you are the kind of organized person that actually writes down your mental lists or you prefer to simply remember each item, lists are extremely helpful. Making a list of chores for your children can clarify your expectations while teaching them how to use their time wisely. Having an agenda for a business meeting will help everyone to know what to expect as well as to expedite the discussions. When a speaker or preacher provides an outline, it can provide not only clarity but a tool to help the listener remember the salient points.

In response to a very serious question from a few of His disciples, Jesus took them aside and gave them a list of very important things for them to remember in the coming days. As He described things that would be happening both in the immediate future and in the distant future, He also gave them some very clear instructions. It must have felt overwhelming to those disciples to hear about the destruction of their temple, but even more to learn that they could be facing intense persecution and enormous world upheaval of all kinds. Yet at the same time, Jesus gave them enormous comfort and hope because He reassured them that one day the Son of Man will come in all His power and glory to establish His eternal kingdom. One day they will be saved. Isn't it interesting that He gave them a list of things to do and to be aware of while they waited for that day?

Do you think that we are actually experiencing some of the events that Jesus described so long ago and that the fulfillment of these prophecies might mean that Jesus will be coming again quite soon? If so, it may be a good idea to check out His list of instructions!

Read Mark 13: 1 - 27

Your thoughts:

THE PROBLEM WITH

SELF -CONFIDENCE

Would you agree that self-confidence is a highly valued trait in our culture? Who comes to your mind when you think of someone who displays this characteristic? A self-confident person trusts his own capabilities and usually has the courage to move ahead even when the outcome is not completely predictable. People who feel self-assured often rise to positions of leadership and prominence. They are eager to reach their goals and to accomplish the tasks that they set out to do. They may or may not be aware of the feelings of other people or the realities that could limit them. They often have a need or a desire to be in control of their environment or situation.

As you read the stories about Peter in the Gospels, he seemed to be a very self-confident person. He was certainly able to express himself, to ask questions of Jesus, to provide leadership, and to declare his unswerving loyalty to his teacher. Apparently he was the only one who did not disappear after Jesus was arrested. You could also say that his self-confidence got him into big trouble. When cornered by the servant girl, his own sense of confidence and courage failed him. In that moment of failure, Peter may have begun to understand that his own strength was not great enough to do what was right. It could well be that as he heard the rooster crow and he broke down and wept in repentance, he became aware in a new way of His need for Jesus. We know that in the coming years Peter found his confidence coming from his relationship to Jesus rather than from himself.

How would you describe yourself?

SELF-confident or GOD-confident?

Read Mark 14: 27 - 31 and Mark 14: 66 - 72

Your thoughts:

LOVE WITHOUT LIMITS

Are these words familiar to you?

"His love has no limits,
His grace has no measure,
His power has no boundary
known unto men.

For out of His infinite riches in Jesus,
He giveth, and giveth,
and giveth again."

They were penned and set to music by Annie Johnson Flint (1866-1932). It was because of a life of loss and illness, tragedy and poverty that Annie shared with us her deep conviction that it was out of His limitless love that Jesus came to this earth. He didn't make up excuses for staying in the comfort of His heavenly home. He didn't delay coming when His Father sent Him. He didn't ask for a substitute or another option. He didn't offer up another suggestion or need an organizational chart. He didn't veer from the plan that the Father always had in His mind - the plan to send Him as a Redeemer and Savior for the people who were in bondage

What made Jesus willing to not only come to this earth as a human baby, giving up the rights and privileges of His equality with God, but willing to become obedient to death, even death on a cross? (Philippians 2: 6 - 8) It could only be because of His love for you and me, for all peoples - His love that is without any limits. It can be called extravagant or lavish love, but our limited vocabulary cannot quite convey the depth of it. It is as we look at the cross that the extent of His love begins to dawn on our consciousness.

"Oh the deep, deep love of Jesus - vast, unmeasured, boundless, free! Rolling as a mighty ocean in its fullness over me!

Underneath me, all around me, is the current of His love.

Leading onward, leading homeward to His glorious rest above."

Read Mark 15 : 14 - 39

Your thoughts:

THE GOOD NEWS

Sometimes it feels like our world is filled with only bad news - crime, hatred, divorce, war, unemployment, earthquakes, persecution, scams and schemes, cheating, and hunger - causing many to feel apathetic, depressed and hopeless. Some people would say that the future looks grim both economically and politically. Others find the moral decay to be extremely upsetting. Do you know of a place where there is good news and hope?

The disciples and followers of Jesus must have been extremely sad and discouraged after they saw and heard that Jesus had actually been found guilty in the mind of Pilate and His accusers and had been hung on a cross while Barabbas was set free. Was there any good news or hope in their minds or conversation as they processed the reality of their situation? Some may have recalled Jesus' mysterious words about "being betrayed, put to death, and then rising again in 3 days", but apparently they did not really grasp that in these ideas there was going to be a future that would be amazing. Actually in the very near future they would not only see the risen Messiah again, but they would become part of God's plan to bring the Good News, the Gospel, everywhere. Their Messiah, their Savior would truly be alive again!

Who needs to hear this Good News from you? Who is ready to hear from you that Jesus is waiting to bring His forgiveness, His love, and His peace to everyone who will believe in Him?

Read Mark: 16: 1 - 20

Your thoughts:

Thoughts from the series called

GOD'S YELLOW LIGHT

Exploring what it means to "wait on the Lord"

in the Old and the New Testament

By Marilyn Miller for

www.westudytogether.com

ANXIETY or ANTICIPATION?

Did you know that researchers tell us that for most people "anticipation is half the fun of any experience"? Whether it be the celebration of Christmas, a family vacation, seeing a friend, or simply one's favorite treat at grandma's house, children and adults alike find pleasure in thinking about the joy that is going to be theirs when the big day comes. While the waiting period might seem long, we often realize that the thinking, the planning and perhaps the dreams have all become part of the actual experience.

Perhaps that is one reason why people of faith have often spoken of the joy that is theirs as they "wait on the Lord". Remember the story of Joseph's life in the Old Testament? He certainly knew what it was to experience extreme disappointment and enormous challenges throughout his years, but he also seemed to grasp that there was a God who was watching over him all along the way and that His Jehovah was with him. Even in the tough times, Joseph waited patiently and expectantly for the Lord to provide for him. When he was given the power to interpret dreams, he always acknowledged that "it was beyond his power to do it, but God could do it through him." Even Pharoah recognized that there was "no one else so obviously filled with the spirit of God." (Genesis 41: 38) Could it be that it was Joseph's humble dependence on God whether he was unfairly serving time in prison or surprisingly appointed to be in charge of the entire land of Egypt, that his readiness to listen to God, to wait on the Lord, enabled him to live to know his grandchildren and to assure them that without a doubt "God would come to help them and lead them back to the land He had solemnly promised to their forefathers".

What does "waiting on the Lord" mean? Surely it includes the willingness to bow down before Him and say, "not my will, but Thine". Certainly it includes the desire to say, "Show me Your way, O Lord. Teach me Your paths." Sometimes it might mean acknowledging that you do not understand the whys of your circumstances, but that you want to put your hope and trust in His goodness and His faithfulness even as you wrestle with your questions and doubts. The anticipation that His mercies will be new every morning will bring peace and joy to your heart and soul as you learn what it means to "wait on the Lord."

Read Psalm 27: 13-14, Lamentations 3: 22-26,

Philippians 3: 20 - 4:1

Your thoughts:

ADDICTED TO WORRY?

What would you say are your biggest worries? Are there concerns that plague your mind in the middle of the night or keep you from focusing well on your work?   Surveys generally agree that the most common worries of Americans include getting old, financial issues and the future, fitness and weight, relational issues, and fatigue or health. What and who do you think about when you have quiet moments of reflection? It is often when we are waiting for information or a solution to a dilemma or for others to make a decision that worry creeps in our minds and hearts.

Do you think that there is an alternative to living captive to our worries and concerns?   Andrew Murray, a well known pastor and writer in the late 1800's, tells us that "If any are inclined to despond, because they do not have such patience, let them be of good courage. It is in the course of our feeble and very imperfect waiting that God Himself, by His hidden power, strengthens us and works out in us the - patience of the great saints, the patience of Christ Himself."   The very same truth, Murray suggests, can be found in Romans 12: 2. "Don't copy the behavior and customs of this world, but let God transform you into a new person by changing the way you think. Then you will learn to know God's will

for you, which is good and pleasing and perfect."
(NLT)

What do you think might change or happen if you decided to turn your greatest anxiety into an active anticipation of the things that God has planned for you and those whom you love? After all, He is the only One who knows the future!

Read Isaiah 40: 27-31,

John 14: 25 - 27, James 5: 7 -8

Your thoughts:

Really? REALLY?

What do you do when you are facing the possibility of unexpected loss? When life is going smoothly and suddenly you find out that your job might end or that medical tests might show cancer? When you know that God is asking you to do something that feels like a foolish risk to you, to whom do you turn? What do you do?

It couldn't have been easy for Abraham when God came to him and asked him to take his only son, Isaac, up to the mountain and sacrifice him as a burnt offering. This was the miracle baby that God have given to him and to Sarah in their old age. This was the promised son through whom God's promises and covenant would be fulfilled. Why in the world would God ask him to do this? But, we read in Genesis 22, Abraham got up early and went with Isaac, wood, fire, and knife in hand. When Isaac asked him about the sheep which they would need, he could tell him with confidence that "God would provide". How did he know this? The habit of worship, of bowing down before the Lord, the Eternal God, in submission and thanksgiving, was his practice. No doubt Isaac had observed how his dad waited on the Lord and Abraham knew that as he waited on his God with faith, that somehow He would keep His covenant promises to them and to his descendants.

We long for everything to go smoothly and according to our plans. God longs for us to allow Him to change our plans and then to watch Him provide for us in miraculous ways and to bless us. It was true for Abraham and Isaac and it is just as true for you and me.

Read Genesis 21: 32 - 22: 19

Your thoughts:

HALF FULL or HALF EMPTY?

There is an old expression that is often used to describe a person's general outlook on life. It is a question that is simple to answer, but it can be quite profound in its implications. The response often indicates whether life is lived with an optimistic or a pessimistic attitude. Of course, the question or saying is, "Is the glass half full or half empty?" Seeing the glass half full lends itself to a very positive outlook, eager to recognize that what you do have is good and worthwhile. It stirs up a grateful spirit and an eagerness to see what might be coming in the future. When one looks at the glass as half empty, the focus stays on what is missing and what might have been if things had turned out differently. It ignites the smoldering embers of discontent into a very negative approach.

When God came to Noah and talked with him about the wickedness and corruption that was in the world at that time, Noah was ready and willing to "do everything as the Lord commanded him." Apparently his close fellowship with God, enabled him to realize that he could trust God with the outcome of what appeared to be an extraordinarily unusual assignment - "Build a large boat." Noah could have been a "half-empty" kind of person, questioning and even resisting the whole idea. Instead, he eagerly went to work, shared his excitement with his wife and boys, and spent his days anticipating what God was going to do in the months and years ahead. Then when he was on the boat and the flood waters were swirling around them, he continued to "wait on the Lord with eager expectation". He was willing to believe that God would care for them and bless them.

It matters not whether you are in the adventuresome stage of "building your boat", waiting and wondering what God is going to do when the boat is complete or living on the boat, waiting and wondering if the storm will ever end, the big question is still "is your glass half full or half empty?"

Read Genesis 6: 5 - 9: 17

Your thoughts:

A PEP TALK

Would you agree that when Christopher Robin said to Winnie the Pooh, "If ever there is tomorrow when we're not together, there is something you must always remember. You are braver than you believe, stronger than you seem, and smarter than you think. But the most important thing is, even if we're apart, I'll always be with you", that he was giving him a "pep talk"? Coaches, teachers, and parents usually become experts at giving these short speeches that are meant to instill enthusiasm and bolster the morale of their children or students. Leaders of all kinds use "pep talks", which are defined as brief, intense, emotional talks that are designed to influence or encourage the audience, to inspire others to work harder and to think positively about themselves and their challenge.

When the Lord spoke to Joshua as he took over from Moses the challenge of leading the Israelites into the Promised Land, He gave him something like a pep talk. There was a huge difference between what the Lord told Joshua, however, and any other kind of human encouragement or inspirational ideas. When God Himself reminded Joshua of His very own presence and strength, it was no longer up to Joshua to believe in himself. He would not be alone. He didn't need to muster up faith in his own abilities or experience. The Lord God promised that "He would be with him. He would not fail or abandon Him. He would give him success." What did Joshua need to do in order to succeed? God made it very clear. "Meditate on His book and do what it says!"

Feeling a little insecure or inadequate? Wishing that someone could give you some additional courage? Why not take the advice that God gave to Joshua and focus on His promises to you. As the Lord said to the Apostle Paul, "My grace is all you need. My power works best in weakness." (2 Cor. 12: 9)

Read Joshua 4: 19 - 24
and Joshua 5; 13 - 8:2

Your thoughts:

IS PATIENCE A VIRTUE?

It seems like the words "waiting" and "patience" have an inextricable bond. A person can wait without patience, of course, but it then becomes a miserable experience and time seems to move even more slowly. Often grumbling, complaining, and frustration are both inwardly felt and outwardly expressed when someone cannot find the strength to be long-suffering. Patience is defined as the capacity to have a "calm spirit" in spite of delays and difficulties. Everyone admires the person who can pleasantly endure a trying situation or person and remain hopeful and optimistic. Usually this happens because of the willingness to understand, to accept, and to look for some positive outcome in the future.

There are times in our lives, just as it has been throughout history, when God asks His children to wait patiently for His intervention and for His perfect timing. It was enormously difficult for Hannah (I Samuel 1) to patiently wait for the child that she longed to have. She was a godly women who prayed faithfully to the Lord but the years went by without the answer that she was seeking. The wait was long and hard, but AT THE RIGHT TIME, God did answer her prayers by giving her a baby boy whom she named Samuel. Her persistent and patient waiting brought her great joy, didn't it? Joy in having a son of her own for several years and then great joy and peace in giving that young boy back to God to serve Him for the rest of his years which was her act of worship and thanksgiving.

God knows and sees the anguish of our hearts when we cry out to Him. It can feel like He is unwilling to respond to our earnest requests, but He also knows and sees what will be the best for us. He longs to satisfy our desires in ways that will cause us to worship and glorify Him beyond our imagination. Patience will always be worth it!

Read I Samuel 1: 1 - 2: 11

Your thoughts:

YOUR EPITAPH

Do you ever think about the kind of epitaph that your family or you might want to have on your tombstone? It can be an entertaining topic of conversation and it can also be quite thought provoking. While the words describing King Ahab were not simply inscribed on stone, they were printed in the Bible for generations of people to read and to consider. It was written that "he did evil in the Lord's sight even more than any of the kings before him" and "he did more to provoke the anger of the Lord, the God of Israel, than any of the other kings of Israel before him." Why in the world did God let such a man rule His people for 22 years? Where was God during the decades when these wicked men ruled the nation of Israel? When would the Lord, the God of Israel, bring judgment upon the wicked and show His mighty power on behalf of those who had been faithful to Him? How long would they have to wait?

When God did decide that the time was right, he used a man with very strong convictions. He asked a man whose name meant, "The Lord is my God" to demonstrate to everyone that his God was alive. He chose a man whose background was insignificant. A man who was not highly educated or refined. A man who had days of incredible faith and courage and had periods of discouragement and weakness. He used a man who would take great risks because he believed with all his heart and soul that his God would answer prayer and bring honor to Himself alone. His name was Elijah.

Wouldn't it be amazing to have it said about you, as it is said about Elijah, "He did as the LORD told him to do"? It's not the size or fame of the miracle, is it? It's the fact that God can use you to demonstrate the power of His resurrection in ways that are ordinarily unexplainable when you are willing to "wait on Him" with conviction.

Read I Kings 18

Your thoughts:

REAL PEACE

Would you agree that being "open-minded" and "tolerant" are character traits that are highly admired these days? No one wants to be labeled as opinionated or politically incorrect. The result is that if you have strong beliefs about life, truth, or morals, either you may have to keep them to yourself or run the risk of being criticized or perhaps even ostracized. As our culture becomes more enamored with the "anything goes" and "just go with the flow" philosophy, it will undoubtedly become more challenging for Christ-followers to take a stand for their Biblically-centered convictions.

Do you think it was any easier in the time of Daniel? When he was chosen to go to the palace to be trained for royal service under King Nebuchadnezzar, Daniel made a life-impacting decision. It was a decision that meant he could live at peace with his God and with himself. He purposed in his heart that he would not pray to any other God or defile himself in any way. (Daniel 1: 8) He was willing to take a new name and to be involved in the pagan education, but he would not partake in the king's food because for him that was a moral choice, reflecting his willingness to participate in the rituals of idol worship. The result of this choice, while it was not easy, was that God blessed Daniel and his 3 loyal friends in wonderful ways. As they waited on the Lord for wisdom, for protection, and for God's name to be revered, they certainly had no idea what the outcome would be, but in the waiting their inner peace was enormously impressive. Daniel's friends even told the king that they knew "the God whom they served was able to save them, but if he did not choose to do so, they would never serve his gold statue or any other gods." (Daniel 3: 16 - 18)

There is a gospel song which was written by P.P. Bliss in 1873, that says,

Dare to be a Daniel.
Dare to stand alone!
Dare to have a purpose firm!
Dare to make it known!

Your resolve today will help you make the right decision tomorrow when your faith and commitment to God is being challenged!

Read Daniel 1 - 6

Your thoughts:

"ALL I HAVE NEEDED"

It's easy to sing the beloved and famous hymn, "Great is Thy Faithfulness" when life is going smoothly, isn't it? The reality of God's compassion and mercy is very clear to us during those periods of time and we are able to express our gratefulness to the Lord from morning to evening. However, what do you do when things look bleak? Sometimes we are prepared for really sad news, serious illness, economic disaster, or a broken relationship, but often it comes as a shock and a huge and devastating disappointment? What songs come to your mind then?

When Jeremiah, God's prophet to the people of Israel, wrote about the suffering of his people as well as his own lament, he said, "Peace has been stripped away and I have forgotten what prosperity is. Everything I had hoped for from the LORD is lost!" (Lamentations 3: 17 - 18) He very clearly expressed his despair and grief, but aren't you thankful that he didn't stop there? He went on to say, "YET I still dare to hope when I remember this: The faithful love of the Lord never ends!" He reminded himself that every day God would be his salvation. There would be new mercies from the Lord each new morning. God's blessings are never early or late. His unfailing love comes to those who wait quietly and submit to His will and His ways.

It is in the unhurried moments and minutes of life, as we wait on Him, that Jesus most often comes to us with His presence and His reassurance that His mercies will never cease. It is in the stillness that we discover that our hope is in Him alone. It is as we quietly trust in His love that we can join in and sing, "Great is Thy faithfulness, O God MY Father. Morning by morning new mercies I see. All I have needed Thy hand has provided. Great is Thy faithfulness, Lord, unto ME!

Read Lamentations 3: 19 - 33

Your thoughts:

THE GIFT of FRIENDSHIP

How many really dear friends do you have that are either about a decade younger or older than you are? The gift of friendship between people in different stages of life is a relationship that is to be treasured and protected. The counsel of a friend like this enriches not only the life of the younger person, but brings strength and purpose to the one with more years of experience. This kind of friendship is a great encouragement to both people as not only wisdom and perspective but enthusiasm and excitement are shared with each other.

There could be several reasons that Mary went quickly to visit Elizabeth after the angel came and told her about the baby that she would conceive by the Holy Spirit. It was a friendship between a young woman and an older woman, but together they shared the biggest events that each of them would ever experience - the birth of miraculous babies. Imagine them talking about the intricacies of becoming pregnant, about the miracle of the baby who would be born to them, about Joseph and his dilemmas and Zechariah's hopes and dreams for his son, and about what they were experiencing during these months of waiting. There is no question that the response that Elizabeth gave to Mary upon her arrival must have given Mary an enormous amount of confidence. To think that her friend accepted her news and recognized her faith without a doubt caused Mary to sing out with joy and certainty to God, her Savior.

How many times in the coming months do you think Mary repeated the words of the song of praise that she sang in the presence of Elizabeth? Together they no doubt encouraged each other as they "waited on the Lord" for the birth of their sons. To have a good friend with whom you can talk about your questions and your concerns as well as your excitement and joys is a wonderful gift from a loving God.

Read Luke 1: 26 - 56 and Luke 2: 1 - 21

Your thoughts:

DELAY or DENIAL?

For generations the people of Israel had been waiting for their Messiah. Centuries of wondering. Centuries of hoping and trusting. Would God keep His promises? Would He really send The One who would rescue them and set up the throne of David and establish His Kingdom? In every century and in every generation there were always the faithful few who did not forget the LORD their God and who continued to walk in His ways, keeping His command to love Him with all their heart and soul and mind and strength. It was only those few who were prepared to recognize this Savior when God did keep His promise. Those few had never stopped waiting and watching because they believed God.

One of those faithful and devout people was Simeon and another was a lady named Anna. Throughout their lifetime each of them had been strong in their faith and unwavering in their convictions. They apparently knew that to live expectantly, anticipating that God would keep His promises to them and to their people, was their mission in life, so they continued to wait with hope and confidence for that day. They knew what David meant when he repeatedly said in his psalms of response to his God, "It is good to wait on the Lord and to put your trust in the Lord." Can you even imagine the level of their joy when they recognized they had had the great privilege of seeing the Messiah, the one who would bring deliverance to all people?

Someone has aptly said, "Never think that God's delays are God's denials." John Ortberg reminds us that "Waiting is not just something we have to do until we get what we want from the Lord. Waiting is part of the process of becoming what God wants us to be." How willing are you to live in expectant hope and patient waiting on the Lord so that He can accomplish His desires in your life and bring glory and honor to His holy name?

Read Luke 2: 21 - 39

Your thoughts:

Thoughts from the series called

WHAT'S ON YOUR MIND?

Exploring what it means to "have the mind of Christ"

By Marilyn Miller for

www.westudytogether.com

WHO'S IN CONTROL?

What is your favorite chapter in the Bible? What chapter would you say is the most important one in all of Scripture? Many theologians and pastors choose Romans 8 because in those 39 verses Paul explained to the Romans the essence of what their faith in Jesus really meant. He gave them the assurance that no matter what struggles, disappointments or challenges they were facing, there was NO CONDEMNATION for those who were in Christ Jesus. He explained to them that the law was no longer their master, but that the Spirit of Christ now lived in them and would bring them the freedom and power to live according to His desires. It's an amazing chapter that is full of promises that have sustained believers throughout the centuries.

Why is it then that you and I seem to be unable to live our lives in complete submission to the Holy Spirit? For example, you envision in the early morning hours a day when you will be patient with your children, kind to your neighbors, at peace with your circumstances, and truthful at all times. In fact, you are quite determined to make this happen. It's a good way to start the day. The reality is that so often old habits or selfish desires pull you away from your goals. Or perhaps the unrest and attitudes of your friends or acquaintances influence your thinking in negative ways. At other times, there is no question that Satan distracts you with taunting thoughts and serious doubts.   It is exactly at that point of discouragement, struggle or failure, when you and I need to return to Romans 6 - 8. We are in good company because even Paul described his own experiences of frustration and need, as well as the remedy for our dilemmas. When parents watch their toddler begin to change from crawling to walking, there are many moments of stumbling, falling, and even going back to crawling again. What is the response of the adults? Punishment and scolding. Never. It is one of love that reaches out a hand, expresses verbal encouragement, and silent adoration. The young child feels that and tries again and again to be like those who adore him.

In some ways, that is just what God the Father is doing for His children when we fall and struggle, isn't it?   He says to you and to me, "The Spirit of God, who raised Jesus from the dead, lives in you. And just as God raised Christ Jesus from the dead, He will give life to your mortal bodies by this same spirit living within you" - Romans 8: 11 NLT   By faith, you and I can learn to be controlled by the Spirit of God who lives in us rather than by our sinful nature - but it will always be step by step by step - one moment at a time.

Read Romans 8: 1 - 17

Your thoughts:

113

CHOOSING METAMORPHOSIS

What would happen if a caterpillar had the opportunity to decide whether or not it wanted to become a moth or a butterfly? Some would, no doubt, refuse to change out of fear or anxiety about the unknown. Others might want to simply be in charge of their own destiny. There may be a few who would look around them and be willing to change if they could be assured that life as a butterfly would be comfortable, easy, and convenient. There may be some who would simply be complacent or disinterested and so they would never really make the choice that is their right and their privilege. If this were true, not only would this be personal loss for the caterpillar, but our whole environment would suffer in a variety of ways.

It is very interesting to note that in Romans 12, Paul urges the believers to "offer their bodies as a living sacrifice to God" and to "let God transform them through changing or renewing their minds". The word _transform_ is actually related to the word _metamorphosis_. Through this process, a gradual change which occurs on the inside will in due time produce a total transformation. That's exactly what God wants to do for us. He gave us "the mind of Christ" through the Holy Spirit who indwells us when we came to Him in repentance and faith. The process of transformation occurs as we yield ourselves to become the person that He intends for us to be, by His mercy and grace.

The thought of change can be scary. For some people it is hard to relinquish their own control or the control which they perceive that they have. At other times the world and the people around us cause us to be confused about the things that are really important. Often we are simply lulled into apathy, indifference or self-satisfaction. What do you think it would take for you to experience the kind of transformation that would bring great glory to the Savior? And great satisfaction and joy to you!

Read Romans 12

Your thoughts:

WHAT MOTIVATES YOU?

What would you say are the best ways to motivate people to change, to do their best, or to accomplish specific goals? At work, a sense of accomplishment, feeling appreciated, and a salary, all impact an employee's motivation level. At home, a sense of shared goals, a cooperative spirit, and defined responsibilities can inspire family members. In the world of education, athletics or the arts, the idea of self-improvement or expression, competition, or the thrill of accomplishment or success can bring people the energy and enthusiasm to do amazing things. One of the enormous challenges for parents, employers, and leaders is to discover what will actually help to motivate individuals because everyone responds in his/her own unique way to incentives that are offered to them.

From the beginning of time, God knew what would inspire the ones that He had created. He walked with them and He talked with them and He shared His deep love for them in that garden setting. When sin entered the world, their lives changed, but God did not. Throughout time God has deeply loved the world. He expressed that love in a visible and tangible way by sending His Only Son, Jesus. He didn't stop there. That Son would be the means by which He could forgive their sinful behavior and their rebellion and bring them back into an intimate and loving relationship with Him. It's a love that is far bigger than our mind can comprehend or our emotions can fully experience - Ephesians 3: 14 - 19. It is that love that, beyond all other human experience, will reach down into the hearts of a person and forever change his/her life.

Knowing this creates a freedom for Paul to clarify some of the changes that God wants to make in the minds and lives of His beloved children. He does not want them to have a new list of commandments or rules or simply unattainable demands, but rather such a deep sense of His love that the deepest desire of their hearts will be to "let the Spirit make them new in the attitude of their minds". Is there any greater incentive than to be loved and to love?

Read Ephesians 4: 17 - 5: 2

Your thoughts:

RECOGNIZING PESSIMISM

Gloom and doom. Negative thinking. Pessimism. Why is it that some people seem to be programmed to focus more on the chance of failure than success, of sickness than health, of misfortune than progress? Many of us do not like to admit it, but we, too, have a tendency to look at our own personal circumstances, the challenges of our neighbors and friends, and certainly the chaos in our world, and feel a sense of anxiety, hopelessness, and at times even despair. When this happens, it is so easy to let one's imagination start moving or to let one's thoughts drift aimlessly through a maze of "what if's", "could be's", and a variety of complex options and solutions.

When Paul wrote to his dear friends in the city of Philippi, he had every reason to share with them the details and story of his suffering and imprisonment. He could have easily written to them, complaining about the unfairness of his situation or the injustice of his sentence.   He could have focused on his disappointments, discouragement and difficulties. But, instead of self-pity, blame, or cynicism, Paul lived out the very same attitude that he was describing to all those who would read his letter. It was the mind-set of his Lord and Savior, Jesus Christ. It was the life of the Spirit of God changing him from the cantankerous, ambitious, aggressive

Saul to the saint and servant that God wanted him to be. There was nothing more important to this man than "knowing Christ and the power of His resurrection and the fellowship of sharing in His sufferings" -

Phil. 3: 10. He knew that who he would become was determined by the attitude and thoughts that he focused on in His mind.

When your mind is "wandering", where does it go? When the unexpected happens or things are out of control, what are some of the thoughts that spin around in your head? When you hear rumors or have to wait for information or a diagnosis, how do you manage the scenarios that play out in your mind? What's on your mind today? How will those thoughts play out in your conversations and life tomorrow?

Read Philippians 2: 5 - 11 and 4: 4 - 13

Your thoughts:

WHY READ THE MANUAL?

When you buy a new car, one of the most important items that will be in your car is a rather insignificant little book that is usually found in the small storage compartment on the dashboard. You will be able to drive your car without it, but if you want to know about all of the options in your car and how to maintain it well, you will find that the "owner's manual" is not only helpful but indispensable. The difficulty with most of these guides is that it can be hard to find the exact information that you need. The search, however, will be important because you will save time and money in the long run if you can solve your dilemmas. Following the manufacturer's list of "what to do" and "what not to do" is always a wise idea.

The letters that Paul wrote to the believers in various locations could be called "operating manuals", couldn't they? For example, in his letter to the Colossians, Paul reminded them that "God has made them alive with Christ" and that because of this, they are no longer bound to the "basic principles of this world". Those were the spiritual truths that the Colossians needed to know and to understand, but in practical terms, what did that mean for them? What does it mean for us? Paul knew that these believers would have questions about their new life in Christ (Col. 2: 6), so he carefully outlined for them both some of the cautions and the some instructions about what this would mean for them. His letters provided clear and concise directions on how to live out their new life in Christ.

Whether you take heed and follow the warnings and advice in the manual for your new car is your own personal decision. Whatever you decide will have consequences both in the present and in the long term. If this is true for a car, think about the ramifications that there are for life. When you and I "set our minds" on eternal values, it will always make a difference in the way that we live. Isn't it great that we have clear instructions in a book like Colossians to help us know just what kind of actions are recommended and what ones are detrimental to those who have God's Spirit and mind?

Read Colossians 2: 20 - 3: 17

Your thoughts:

SPECTATOR or PARTICIPANT?

If you had your choice, would you rather have tickets for a professional football, basketball, baseball or hockey game? Perhaps you would rather watch golf, tennis or a marathon? You will, no doubt, thoroughly enjoy watching the competition and admire those playing the game, but unless you are actually participating in the event itself, it is not likely that the thrill can compare with the experience of the athletes themselves. Those people who deliberately made choices that enabled them to improve their skills, keep their focus, and reach some of the goals that they clearly had in mind, are the ones who have the privilege of feeling a real sense of accomplishment and success.

There is a big difference between those who participate in an event and those who observe, isn't there? Between those who get actively involved and those who are content to stand on the sidelines where it seems to be safe and secure. Between those who decisively dedicate themselves to practice, to learn from their mistakes, and to improve their competency and those who "take it easy". Peter, in his letter to the believers who are experiencing so many trials and persecution, explains clearly to them that it is very important for each one of them to be dedicated and decisive in thinking and perspective so that they could live out before the world the holiness of Jesus.   That's a rather amazing challenge, isn't it? Is it possible?

If you thrive on thrills, action, and impossibilities, then Peter has the experience of a lifetime waiting for you to explore. If you are more attracted to a slow and steady pace, then Peter has some recommendations that will be suited to your taste as well. If you know that your coordination is limited or you feel somewhat handicapped, Peter understands that, too. So there is really no excuse! Don't put it off until tomorrow. There is nothing that exceeds the joys that God has promised to those who participate eagerly and actively in the almost unbelievable challenge to "be holy because He is holy".   Wow! "Let the game begin."

Read I Peter 1: 1 - 21

Your thoughts:

ABOUT THE AUTHOR

Marilyn Miller has always loved teaching. She majored in education and Christian education at Wheaton College. For several years she was the Director at an enrichment center for preschoolers. In recent years God has blessed her desires by giving her the opportunity to lead a women's Bible study and to write all of the studies for this group of enthusiastic participants.

Marilyn loves hospitality, reading, travel, walking, and most of all her family which includes her husband, Fred, 3 daughters and their husbands and families.

Keep up with Marilyn on:

Westudytogether.com

Women-in-the-word.com

Made in the USA
San Bernardino, CA
13 February 2018